GOD'S HANDS & FEET

by Lisa Soland

Illustrated by
Gareth Brookshire

God's Hands & Feet

by Lisa Soland

Illustrated by Gareth Brookshire

Published in 2020 by:
Climbing Angel Publishing
PO Box 32381, Knoxville, Tennessee 37930
www.ClimbingAngel.com

First Edition December 2020
Printed in the United States of America
Cover and Interior Design by Climbing Angel Publishing
A special thanks to Jon Bonjour and Shawn Williams

ISBN: 978-1-64921-808-7

This story is dedicated to Fred,

& his good and kind mother.

GOD'S HANDS & FEET

My mother is good and kind. Out of all the helpful things I've learned about real-life, from all sorts of people, my mother has taught me the most.

Every night my mother tucks me into bed and tells me, "Fred, you are one of God's very important ambassadors."

"What's that mean, Mother?"

"It means that you are being set apart for His purposes."

"Purposes? Like what?"

"You are to be *God's hands and feet* because when He wants to do something good in this world, He sometimes uses us to do it."

She then kisses me goodnight and turns out the light. And I go to sleep with that on my mind.

My mother and father take us boys places. Fun places, *sometimes.* But most of our free time is spent visiting people who need something good from God. Sick people. People who can't get out of the house to buy things they really need. And people who are in the most trouble of all…

…people who have lost hope.

These sick people lie in their beds, sad and unable to move, and my mother sits beside them. She reminds them that God has a great plan, and they are an important part of that plan.

My mother stays there for a long time, much longer than I could. She sits and listens. Then, from time to time, she'll say, "Remember now, you are here for a reason." And the hopeless person gets to breathing easier again.

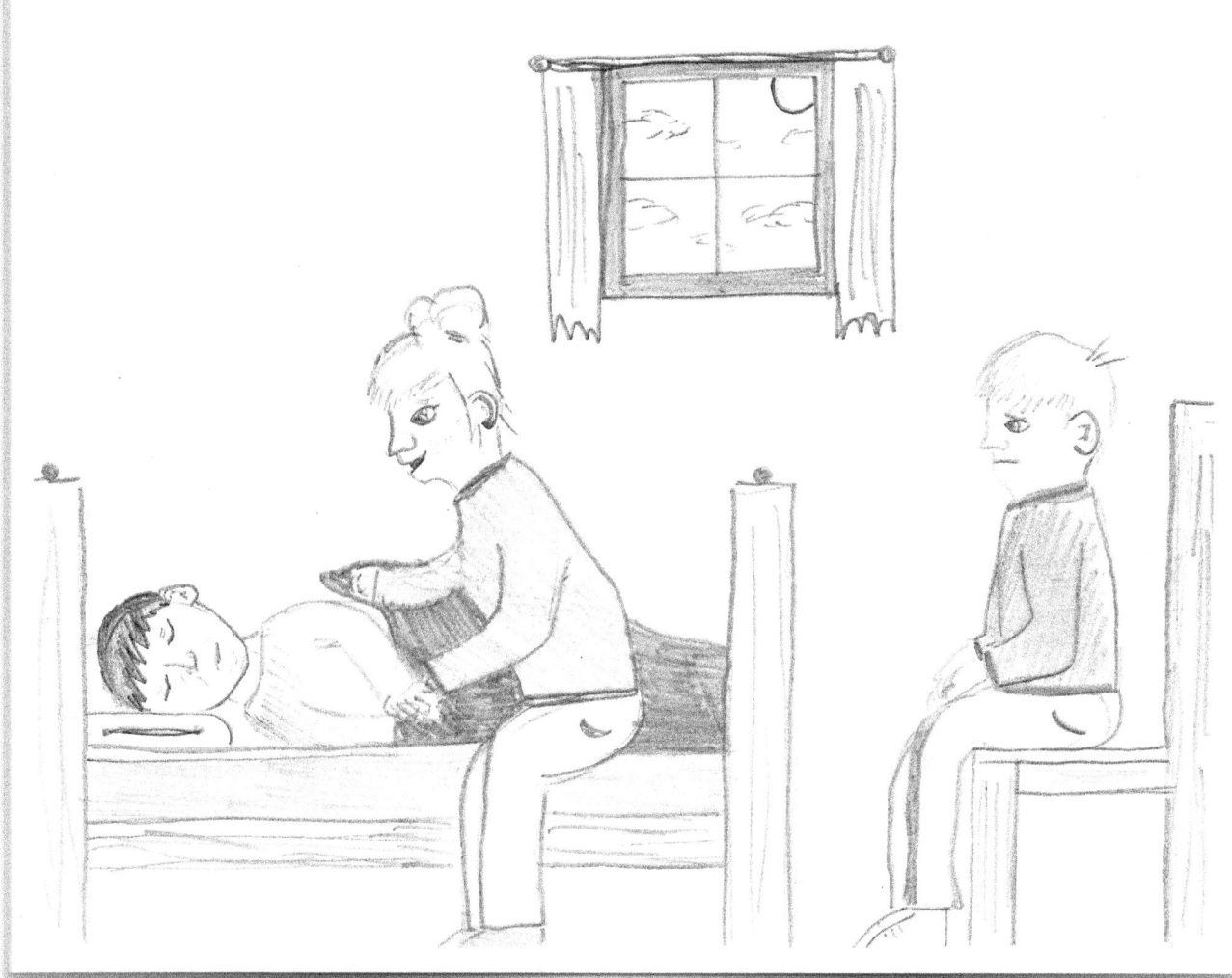

By the time we leave, the sick person has a much happier look on their face, and sometimes they even get out of bed and walk us to the front door.

My brothers and I are encouraged to make friends with children who have no friends. We are also taught the value of befriending those who don't have as many nice things as we do.

There was this boy in my class, and his name was Wayne. He did not have a winter coat. Not one. It doesn't matter in the summer, but this was winter, and it was freezing cold outside.

I often wondered. *How did Wayne do it? How could he walk out his front door, every day, into the freezing cold of winter with icicles falling from the roof, and not wear some sort of heavy jacket?*

But Wayne had nothing, nothing at all to keep him warm.

One Christmas, I got an amazing brand new winter coat. And when our Christmas break was over, I wore that new coat to school, proudly displaying it for all to see. I felt like a million dollars wearing that coat!

Every morning before school, and every afternoon when school was over, I couldn't wait to push my arms through the sleeves of that new coat and button it up. It fit me perfectly, like it had been made exactly for me.

Every day I would arrive at school and hang my new coat on one of the 27 hooks that lined the wall of our seventh-grade classroom.

Then, like clockwork, Wayne would walk over, remove my coat from its hook, and wear it during class. But not just one class, every class. All through the day. Every single day.

Wayne would wear my brand new amazing Christmas coat every single day. I wore it to and from. He wore it all day.

I didn't mind so much, really. In fact, I felt a little bad for the guy, not having a coat of his own.

My mother says that "*feeling bad*" for others is good. It's a sign of compassion, and "*feeling*" compassion is a good thing. But "*doing compassionate acts*" for others is far better than a "*feeling.*"

Every day when school was over, I'd have to ask Wayne for my new coat back.

"Hey, Wayne."

"Hey, Fred."

"It's time to go."

"Yeah."

"I need my coat. Back. Now."

"Yeah, I know."

He would then take off my coat and sadly hand it back to me.

I'm telling you, I hated that part of the day. Hated it. Not sure why, but asking Wayne for my own coat back was the least fun part of my entire day! And I had to do it! Every day!

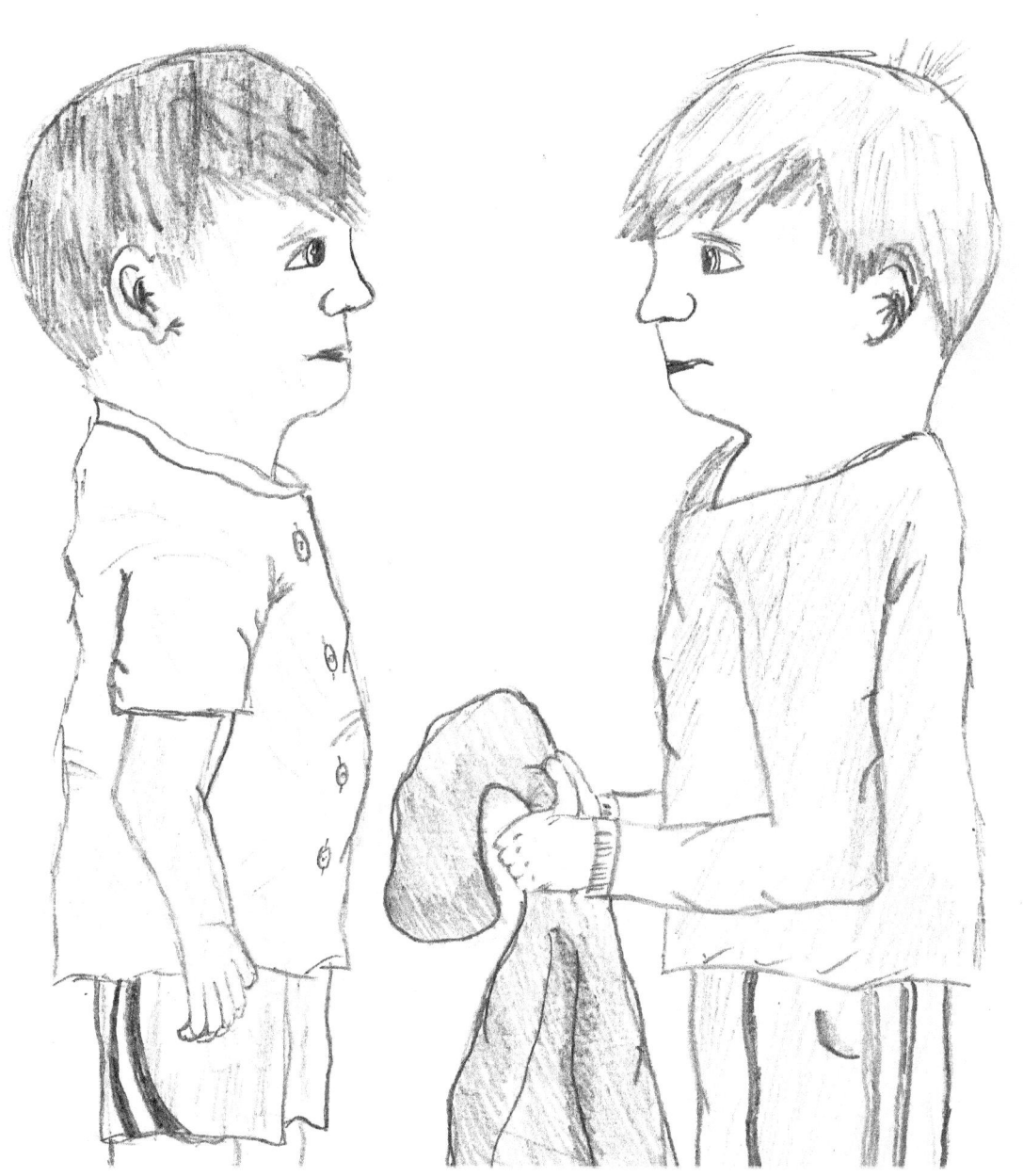

One night after dinner, I pulled my mother aside and explained to her about what had been going on at school with Wayne. I guess I was hoping for her to show *ME* some compassion. But she said something I never expected her to say…ever. She said, "Fred, tomorrow I want you to give that precious little boy your new coat."

"What?!"

"Listen, Son. Tomorrow when school is over, and it's time for all of you children to return to your families, I want you to let Wayne keep your coat."

"But Mom, what will I wear?!"

She walked over to the hall closet and pulled out my *old* winter coat, and said, "You'll wear this, Fred. It still fits you fine, and it will keep you plenty warm. You give that precious boy your *new* coat."

"How 'bout I give him my *old* coat?" I asked. "My old coat could keep *him* plenty warm too."

"He doesn't want your *old* coat. He wants your *new* one."

I was confused. My mother had given me *that new coat*. And now she's telling me to give it to someone else.

"I'm confused," I told her.

"Well, that's to be expected, Fred. Sometimes we don't fully understand the importance of *giving* until after we've gone ahead and done it."

I love my mother, but sometimes she takes me for a loop. But there is no denying; she is good and kind. And some part of me, deep down inside myself, wanted to be just like her. So, even though I didn't want to, I did what she said.

The next day when it came time for all of us kids to go home, Wayne came over to me, and without me even asking this time, he began to take off my new coat.

I said quickly, "Wayne, it's yours. You can have it." (I thought I'd better say it fast before I changed my mind.)

"What?!" he asked as if he was absolutely astounded at what he had heard.

I repeated slowly, "You, can, have, my, new, coat."

"But Christmas is over," he said.

"Not for God."

And with that, I helped him put my new coat back on, which was now his, for keeps. I even helped him button up those buttons.

When he was fully dressed in the new coat, Wayne said, "Geez, Fred. I feel like a million dollars," and he started to cry.

I didn't know what to do at first. Then I thought I'd better go ahead and let him because it was freezing outside, and Wayne was starting to realize that he wasn't going to have to be cold anymore.

Wayne always sat by himself on the bus. I figured he thought he wasn't good enough to sit beside any of the other boys…boys who had lunch boxes with good food inside for them to eat at lunchtime…boys with happy faces and full stomachs.

Boys with coats.

But not *this* day.

On our way home from school *this* day, Wayne sat next to *me*. And we've been the best of friends ever since.

When God wants to do something good, sometimes He needs *us* to do it. Sometimes it's hard to do good—to give up something of real value. And sometimes it's not so hard. But if God's behind it, it's **always good**. And something better than you can ever imagine happens because of it —like getting a lifelong best friend.

Start children off on the way they should go,

and even when they are old they will not turn from it.

(Proverbs 22:6 NIV)

THE END

ABOUT CLIMBING ANGEL PUBLISHING

Climbing Angel Publishing exists for the purpose of sharing stories of hope and encouragement, aiding in the gathering together of community, and supporting the process of betterment. The following books are available at ClimbingAngel.com and major bookstores.

ADULT BOOKS: (Romans 8:28-30)

In His Image, Sam Polson (English, Romanian, & Mandarin)
By Faith, Sam Polson (English & Romanian)
My Birthday Gift to Jesus, Lisa Soland
Without Ceasing, Dr. Dennis Davidson
SonLight: Daily Light from the Pages of God's Word, Sam Polson
Corona Victus: Conquering the Virus of Fear, Sam Polson
Art Bushing: His Diary, Letters, & Photographs of WWII, Art Bushing
Art & Dotty: His Diary, Their Letters & Photographs of WWII, Art Bushing
Trimisul, Stan Johnson (available in Romanian only)
Life Changing Prayer, Sam Polson

CHILDREN'S BOOKS: (Philippians 4:8)

The Christmas Tree Angel, Lisa Soland
The Unmade Moose, Lisa Soland
Thump, Lisa Soland
Somebunny To Love, Lisa Soland (English & Mandarin)
The Truth about God's Rainbow, Lisa Soland
God's Promises, Lisa Soland
The Boy and The Bagel Necklace, Lisa Soland
God's Hands & Feet, Lisa Soland
I Like To Be Quiet, Joni Caldwell
Wheels Up!, Karlie Saumier

I LIKE TO BE QUIET
by Joni Caldwell

This book is written to honor *the quiet child*, the child that likes to observe, the child that enjoys a little alone time to think. Like me, I know you are amazed as you watch your quiet child. I hope this book will serve as the backdrop for you to snuggle into each other for a while. Let's make sure they know how interesting they are and how very proud we are of them, *just the way they are.*

GOD'S HANDS & FEET
by Lisa Soland

In *God's Hands & Feet*, Fred's mother teaches him invaluable lessons on how to be "one of God's very important ambassadors." She explains, "You are to be God's hands and feet because when God wants to do something good in this world, He sometimes uses us to do it."

"Start children off on the way they should go, and even when they are old they will not turn from it." (Proverbs 22:6 NIV)

THE BOY & THE BAGEL NECKLACE
by Lisa Soland

In *The Boy and The Bagel Necklace*, Andrew, a resident of a Romanian orphanage, tells us the story of when Jesus visits him in a dream. Jesus tells Andrew not to worry, that everything is going to be all right. Soon after, the leadership in Romania changes and little Andrew is adopted and brought to America where he learns that Jesus Christ is more than just a nice man who visits desperate children in their dreams. When little Andrew learns just how much God loves him, his life is radically changed.

WHEELS OFF!
by Karlie Saumier

Wheels Off! is Hazel and Henry's first of many adventures together. Henry is Hazel's little brother, who sometimes wishes he wasn't so little. While playing at the local playground, a group of bullies pick on Henry, but his sister is there to help him discover that "Heaven on Earth" is not that far away.

"A terrific Christ-inspired story of forgiveness, family, and friendship."
– Lisa Soland, author

Lightning Source UK Ltd.
Milton Keynes UK
UKHW021441041220
374569UK00002B/166